The Gardens
of Stanley Street

This Stanley Street story belongs to…

....

For Balsall Heath Jungle and all
small gardeners everywhere (M.R)

For Gav and Sarah and their garden to be! (S.S)

Published by Birmingham Advisory and Support Service
Balden Road, Harborne, Birmingham B32 2EH

ISBN 1-898244-71-5

Project Co-ordinator: Fran Stevens
Editor: Lorraine Horsley
Designer: Anne Matthews
Text © Mandy Ross 2003
Illustrations © Sami Sweeten 2003

All rights reserved. No part of this publication may be reproduced, stored in a retrieval system, or transmitted in any form or by any means, electronic, mechanical, photocopying, recording or otherwise without the prior written permission of the Publishers.

The Gardens
of Stanley Street

written by Mandy Ross
illustrated by Sami Sweeten

It was grey and gloomy on Stanley Street.

"Let's brighten things up," said Daisy Plum from Number 1. "We could grow our own fruit and vegetables."

So she organised the first ever meeting of the Stanley Street Gardening Club.

"What would you like to grow?" Daisy Plum asked Hotwheels Hugh from Number 2,

Mee-Mee Lee from Number 3,

Noori Shakoor from Number 4,

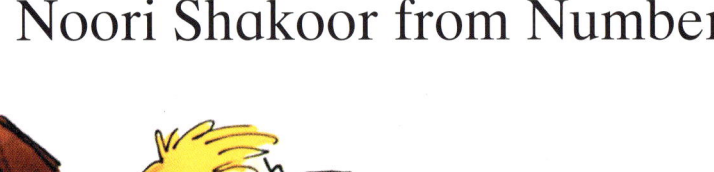

Lively Clive from Number 5,

Trixie Rix from Number 6,

Miss McLeven from Number 7,

the Lately-Thwaites from Number 8

and Ms Rosie O'Toole and the children from Stanley Street School.

They wrote a list:

a cherry tree, an apple tree
a pear tree and a plum tree
strawberry shoots and
raspberry shoots
a juicy-lucy gooseberry bush
red-hot chilli seeds
stripey-sue tomato seeds
quick-quick pumpkin seeds
and a hundred baby beanstalks.

Next Saturday morning, Daisy Plum led a great, green procession down Stanley Street.

Everyone cheered. "Here come our plants!"

There was...

a cherry tree for Daisy Plum,
an apple tree for Hotwheels Hugh,
a pear tree and a plum tree for Mee-Mee Lee,
chilli seeds for Noori Shakoor,
tomato seeds for Lively Clive,
pumpkin seeds for Trixie Rix,
strawberry shoots and raspberry shoots for Miss McLeven,
a gooseberry bush for the Lately-Thwaites,
and a hundred baby beanstalks for Ms Rosie O'Toole at Stanley Street School.

That weekend on Stanley Street, there were
chats and calls over garden walls,
and hints and tips on sowing and growing,
and swapping and sharing and much comparing.

There were gardening boots and gardening hats,
and frisky dogs and hide-away cats,
and digging and delving and potting and planting
of trees and seeds and roots and shoots…

and aching backs, and steaming baths.

In the gardens of Stanley Street, the plants rooted
down through cold snaps and icy winds,
shivery showers and rattling rain,
thunderstorms and lightning, sudden snows and rainbows.

As the days grew warmer,
there were more chats and calls over garden walls,
and weeding together whatever the weather,
and swapping and sharing and much comparing.

At last in Stanley Street, it was SPRING!
There was…

cherry blossom, apple blossom,
pear blossom, plum blossom,
strawberry buds and raspberry buds,
and juicy-lucy gooseberry buds,
red-hot chilli flowers,
stripey-sue tomato flowers,
quick-quick pumpkin flowers…

and a hundred knee-high
beanstalks.

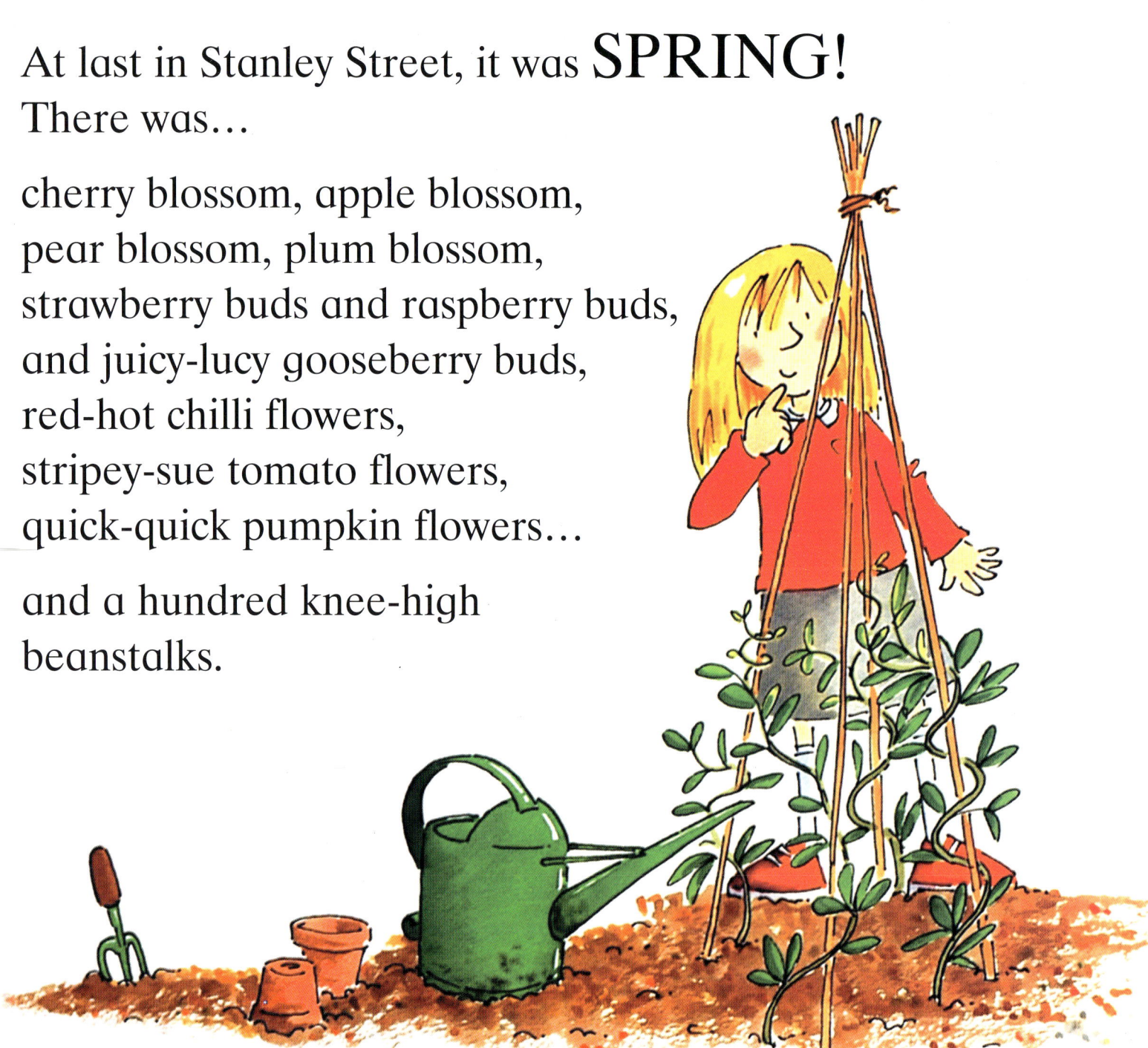

Eating the plants were...

big snails, little snails, big slugs, little slugs, greenfly, whitefly, blackfly and caterpillars.

Catching *them* were...

ladybirds, hedgehogs, big frogs, little frogs, big birds, little birds, and Miss McLeven every evening after rain.

By summer Stanley Street was bursting with…

cherries and apples, pears and plums,

strawberries and raspberries, and gooseberries,

red-hot chilli peppers, stripey-sue tomatoes,

big, fat orange pumpkins

and a hundred beanstalks
as high as the sky.

And butterflies!

And then there were MORE chats and calls over garden walls,
and hints and tips on cooking and baking,
and swapping and sharing and much comparing,
ready for…

the Stanley Street Garden Party!
Along came…

Hotwheels Hugh from Number 2,
Mee-Mee Lee from Number 3,
Noori Shakoor from Number 4,
Lively Clive from Number 5,

Trixie Rix from Number 6,
Miss McLeven from Number 7,
the Lately-Thwaites from Number 8,
and Ms Rosie O'Toole and the
children from Stanley Street School.

And they brought...

cherry tart, apple pie, pear pudding
and plum cake,
strawberry milkshake, raspberry jelly,
and juicy-lucy gooseberry jam,
red-hot chilli curry,
stripey-sue tomato stew,
quick-quick pumpkin pie and a delicious
GIANT-beanfeast.

And Daisy Plum cried, "Three cheers for the Stanley Street gardeners!"

Gardening on YOUR street

The Gardens of Stanley Street was inspired by Balsall Heath Jungle, a community gardening project which encourages people in the city to grow their own fruit and vegetables.

Whether or not you've got a garden, there are lots of ways you can get gardening and grow your own fruit, vegetables and flowers – as well as looking after the environment and encouraging wildlife in your area. Here are some organisations and websites which may be helpful.

Finding information

Ask at your local library for information about city farms and community gardening projects in your area and renting an allotment from your local council. Allotments are public gardens divided into plots where people can grow whatever they want.

Gardening websites with useful information for young gardeners include:
www.gardenadvice.co.uk; www.links4kids.co.uk; www.kidsgardening.com

Useful organisations

The Federation of City Farms and Community Gardens has details about your nearest city farm or community gardening project.
www.farmgarden.org.uk or write to the GreenHouse, Hereford Street, Bristol BS3 4NA

The Organic Network for Schools at the Henry Doubleday Research Association (a research centre for organic gardening) offers information about making a school garden and organic gardening.
www.hdra.org.uk/schools_organic_network or write to HDRA, Coventry, Warwickshire CV8 3LG

The National Trust may have special gardens to visit in your area.
www.nationaltrust.org.uk or write to 36 Queen Anne's Gate, London SW1H 9AS. In Scotland: www.nts.org.uk or write to Wemyss House, 28 Charlotte Square, Edinburgh EH2 4ET

RSPB (Royal Society for the Protection of Birds) works to improve the environment for birds and other wildlife.
www.rspb.org.uk or write to RSPB, The Lodge, Sandy, Bedfordshire SG19 2DL

Groundwork may have a group working in your area to improve the environment.
www.groundwork.org.uk or write to Groundwork, 85-97 Cornwall Street, Birmingham B3 3BY

Friends of the Earth campaigns on local and world environmental issues.
www.foe.co.uk or write to FoE, 26-28 Underwood Street, London N1 7JQ. In Scotland:
www.foe-scotland.org.uk or write to FoE Scotland, 72 Newhaven Road, Edinburgh EH6 5QG

The author

Mandy Ross has written lots of books for children of all ages, including *Peekaboo Baby!* which was shortlisted for the Sainsbury Baby Book Award. She lives with her partner and son, Joe, in Birmingham, which inspired the Stanley Street stories.

The illustrator

Sami Sweeten lives by the seaside and likes cats and growing flowers. When she was little, Sami wanted to draw pictures and make up stories and grow sunflowers. Now she's grown up, she draws pictures, makes up stories and grows all sorts of flowers in her garden! She also collects snails in a bucket.

Stanley Street Story series:

Big books:
Traffic Trouble on Stanley Street
The Gardens of Stanley Street
No Place to Play in Stanley Street Park

Read together story books:
Traffic Trouble on Stanley Street
The Gardens of Stanley Street
No Place to Play in Stanley Street Park

Read alone stories:
Hotwheels Hugh from Number 2
Mee-Mee Lee from Number 3
Noori Shakoor from Number 4
Lively Clive from Number 5
Trixie Rix from Number 6
The Lately-Thwaites from Number 8